CRIES OF THE SOUL

Complete Edition

Tammy Henson

Cries of the Soul

© 2015 by Tammy Henson.

All rights reserved. No part of this book may be reproduced, stored in a retrieval system or transmitted in any form or by any means without the prior written permission of the publishers, except by a reviewer who may quote brief passages in a review to be printed in a newspaper, magazine or journal.

First Printing

Softcover: 978-1542514293

PUBLISHED BY REVIVAL WAVES OF GLORY BOOKS & PUBLISHING

www.revivalwavesofgloryministries.com

Litchfield, IL

Printed in the United States of America

Table of Contents

Dedication 7

Volume One 8

    The Year of the Lord's Favor 9

    His Grace 11

    God Is the Way 12

    Thanksgiving 14

    Happy is the Christmas Heart 16

    "Easter" 18

    "Believe" 20

    Through the Blood 22

    The Devil Took It, God Gives It Back 24

    Angels 26

    Enemy vs. God 27

    Love Is… 29

    "God's Hand" 31

    I Am New 33

    "Enemy No – More" 35

    Forgiveness 37

    "Fear" 39

    "No Trust In Men" 41

    I Love My Children 43

    Falling 45

    Purpose 47

    It's the Darkest Before Dawn 49

Cries of the Soul

- Cry In Trouble 51
- Volume Two 54
  - Son 55
  - My Jess 57
  - Emily 59
  - Loving Zack 61
  - Bay 63
  - Seeds 65
  - Vision 67
  - Power 69
  - Your Way Or Mine 71
  - Sinful Church 73
  - Heaven 75
  - Promise 77
  - Living Bread 79
  - Thoughts of the Word 81
  - Broken 83
  - Amazing Grace 86
  - A Heart for Jesus 88
  - The Enemies Lies 91
  - The Answer 93
  - Breaking Free 95
  - Casting Off 97
  - "Transition" 99
  - I'm a New Me 101
  - My Heart 103
  - My Past Made Me 105

Today's World	107
Giants	109
God's Power	111
His Presence	113
The Desert	115
The Days In a Week	117
Keeping God In a Box	120
The Voices	122
Generation	124
Set Me On Fire	127
The New Me	129
Beautiful Me	131
A Dream Seen	133
Battle Keys	135
Denied By His People	137
Darkness	139
Your Redeemer Lives	142
The World Who Needs God	144
Pain	146
His Loss Our Gain	148
Bad Company	150
The Root	152
Forgive	155
The Church of Lack	157
My Entrusted	159
Fire	161
I Pray	163

Cries of the Soul

Inner Longing 165

This Place 168

Simplicity 170

Sheol 172

Truly Saved 174

DEDICATION

I am dedicating a piece of this book to my children. Whom I love with all my heart and soul. My heart longs for you. You are very special and deserve to be commended for the life you put inside of me. If it wasn't for you I wouldn't be the woman inside of me. Thank you Seth, Jessica, Zack, Emily and Jaden. You are dearly treasured as a rare commodity. Our memories linger and are not forgotten. To all my beautiful children, thank you for being the song of my life.

Tammy Henson

VOLUME ONE

The Year of the Lord's Favor

My stone has been set in place,
    it's like horses in a race.

The time is near,
    for your favor dear.

The light is shining on you,
    so my miracle can come through.

Others will know I am your Lord,
    because of my mighty sword.

I've gathered your treasures, to bring them forth
    I've walked beside you on your course.

The end of the road is almost here,
    pick up your armor and do not fear.

Many will plot against you,
    but they will not win, not matter what they do.

Your getting what you deserve,
    it has been preserved.

What has been stolen, has been found,
    at my anger, I strike in sound.

What has been done,
    doesn't matter because in the end you won.

Cries of the Soul

Open your mouth, tell with your lips,
    what the lord; depicts.

Tell everyone what I've done,
    do not walk but run.

Testify to my mighty power,
    tell them the joy of my spiritual shower.

Tell them of my mercy and love,
    so they too can fly like a dove.

Watch and listen,
    so my glory can glisten.

For the purpose I have for you,
    is to carry others through.

I the Lord love My people,
    and want to put them in my steeple.

Glorify and praise my name,
    because you have no shame.

I sent Jesus to take it all,
    so when you came to me, you wouldn't fall.

Stand up and proclaim,
    I can rescue, the lame.

There's nothing I can't do,
    I can restore, even the darkest of you.

His Grace

His Grace
    reached down and touched my face.

His Grace
    brought me to this glorious place.

His Grace
    found me at a fast pace.

His Grace
    is the only trace.

His Grace
    crowned me as beautiful as lace.

His Grace
    what an embrace.

His Grace
    my number one race.

His Grace
    how I love His
Grace .....

God Is the Way

God is the way
    it's because of Him your alive today.

He rejoiced when you were born
    and He cries when your heart is torn.

Most people don't understand what He's done
    most people just get scared and run.

My mother raised me in God's way
    but as a teenager, my heart didn't stay.

Partying, drinking and doing drugs
    I didn't realize the love in my mother's hugs.

God's been working on me
    He's shaping my heart the way it should be

I wish others could see the light
    I wish they could feel God hugging them so tight.

God is good, God is great
    no more evil, no more hate.

He's here to show you His mercy and grace
    miracles aren't the only trace.

He's showed me so much
    I love His tender touch.

Cries of the Soul

God is the way praise His Name
    show everyone His love and fame.

Turn to Him and He'll help you
    in everything you do.

No more sadness, no more tears
    there is no reason to keep your fears.

His love will never go away

Ask now and receive all He has to give
    He is the way to live.

THANKSGIVING

Thank You Jesus on this Thanksgiving Day
    as we eat and pray.

Thank You Jesus for family and friends
    that you so graciously send.

Thank You Jesus for everything You give
    bless this life we live.

Thank You Jesus on this Thanksgiving Day
    for loving me in every way.

Thank You Jesus for dying for me
    and setting me free.

Thank You Jesus for making me new
    and blessing me in all I do.

Thank You Jesus on this Thanksgiving Day
    and we worship your name today.

Thank You Jesus for all the free gifts
    and the burdens You lift.

Thank You Jesus for healing me
    and turning me into who I need to be.

Thank You Jesus on this Thanksgiving Day
    I just want to say:

All the thanks belongs to you
    for everything you have pulled us through.

HAPPY IS THE CHRISTMAS HEART

God promises from Him we will never part.

Singing, laughing and praying,
    listen carefully to what He is saying.

I am like an eagle in the sky,
    above all I can hear your cry.

I care about all your painful memories,
    I know it hurts like a sting from a bumble bee.

I care about the way people treat you,
    loving and caring is all I do,
    I desire this from you to,

God loves good deeds,
    He will bless you with all your needs.

He brings many things to you in many ways,
    He watches over you every day.

He's in the rainbows, He's in the sky,
    He's the angel passing by.

He is the safety of the hand,
    He is the music in the band,
    He is powerful in His stand.

Being happy or being sad,
> God does not want things to happen so bad.

He is the smile in your soul,
> He will make you joyful and whole.

God can feel your pain,
> His angel is the thunder and the rain.

Sitting under a tree in the Spring,
> Listening to a beautiful bird sing.

Looking up into the sky so clear,
> feeling the Lord is near.

I feel the fire burning inside,
> I feel His precious love that never dies.

Nothing better than a gift of a rose,
> Life itself is a gift so treasure it and keep it close.

Great is the love of the Lord,
> He's constantly knocking at your door.

I truly believe in miracles He gives,
> and the happy life He lets you live.

A beautiful scenery of a dove,
> shows His caring and His love.

If you listen, you can hear His voice.

Do you wanna to burn in hell,
> or do you wanna preach and tell.

Tell the love He has for them,
> Let them know the power in Him.

I'm gonna say towards this poems end,
> think of this message God appointed me to send.

"Easter"

Easter is more than eggs, candy and fun,
    It's the battle that Jesus won.

Through the blood and the cross,
    our sins he tossed.

From Heaven to Earth,
    everyone rejoiced in His birth.

Through His perfect life,
    the blades cut like a knife.

He did it for you, He did it for me,
    He did it, to set us free.

As He died and arose on the third day,
    He made everything possible, in every way.

Through His blood we're forgiven,
    let's celebrate because He has risen.

Oh what a love that must be,
    to suffer for you and me.

He's still here; to intercede on our behalf,
    to have His way as we walk His path.

We are forgiven of our sins each day,
    as we repent and pray.

Remember on this Easter Day,
    He died and arose from the dead, so we don't have to pay.

Rejoice and praise His name,
    because He bled and bore our shame.

"BELIEVE"

Never lose faith just because you can't see,
    God has a plan for you and me.

Every detail is in motion,
    He is preparing the way through the ocean.

Sometimes it's a process, in His perfect plan,
    but in distress, He leads you with His hand.

He walks beside you just in case you didn't know,
    to strengthen and guide you, when you're feeling low.

He's never early, nor ever to late,
    He's right on time, on that perfect date.

Tests and trials are to build you up,
    and you'll be happy when He fills you up.

When your rainbow comes, filled with gold,
    you will know joy of young and old.

Hold on to God's Word, His every decree,
    the truth will set you free.

And always remember the love of the Lord,
    shining with grace, with His mighty roar.

He's always there to lend an ear,
    so talk to Him, He's always near.

He listens and cares,
   all our burdens He bares.

Lean on the Holy Throne,
   and remember you're not alone.

THROUGH THE BLOOD

Thank you Jesus for shedding your blood,
    for the cross immersed in mud.

You suffered and died for me,
    so I could live and be set free.

It's because of You, Your Father accepts me,
    Through You, He sees a precious little bee.

I get honey, shelter and beauty to shine on me,
    so God's love I can see.

You suffered and died,
    so God could hear me when I cried.

He collects every tear,
    and takes away my deepest fear.

Oh how that blood,
    rushed out like a flood.

And when You were nailed,
    nothing else failed.

And with Your last breathe,
    supplying your death.

I was made whole,
    So your spirit could embrace my soul.

Cries of the Soul

And the Glory be to You,
    for everything you do.

Because of you, I am carried through,
    Heaven awaits me, as I live for You.
    I praise You, in the midst of everything I do.

You laid Your life down,
    So I could join the Heavens, in a crown.

Nothing better than the joy you give,
    And because of your blood I live.

And so it is, that through the cross,
    I don't have to suffer any loss.

Thank You Jesus for Your blood shed,
    and the thorns on Your head.

You suffered, so I don't have to,
    that's why I love You.

THE DEVIL TOOK IT, GOD GIVES IT BACK

The Devil has destroyed me,
   nothing left as far as I can see.

Addicted to drugs,
   and now my children I can't kiss or hug.

I lost it all,
   every step I take I fall.

Death awaits,
   but God reached down, and took my hate.

He delivered me,
   and molded me into who he wanted me to be.

Because I obeyed, He gave me joy,
   His Spirit is my toy.

I love Jesus in every way,
   and Here's what He has to say.

What the devil meant for harm,
   I will make my charm.

Hold fast to My promises to you,
   and praise me in all you do.

I will give everything back,
    In its season, you will not lack.

Have faith and pray,
    for victory is coming, in your day.

And remember, no weapon formed against you will prosper.

ANGELS

Angels flying in the sky,
    you may not know it, but one is nearby.

Protecting you in everything you do,
    keeping you from your enemies to.

One is called your guardian angel,
    if you're in danger just yell.

They will hear your plea for help

Angels are everywhere,
    even though seeing them is rare,
    never doubt an angel is there.

Watching over you day and night,
    letting you see that Jesus is the light.

Angels flying in the sky,
    Jesus is what you should try.

Trying to love and trying to care,
    You will find, there is a lot of it there.

Jesus has His angels watching over you,
    and loves you no matter what you do.

ENEMY VS. GOD

The Enemy Came In:

To make my heart week,
    to tell me lies to speak.

To rob my joy and make me hope no more,
    to shut the greatest door.

The enemy came in; to steal,
    to make me an unbelievable deal.

He took away my faith,
    he made tears run down my face.

He put the chains on and held me tight,
    from fear to sadness, this just ain't right.

I found my way back,
    it was hard, this battle; I was under attack.

God showed me, how much I needed Him,
    He showed me my tree and it's broken limb.

He showed me just how much I had,
    How without Him, it gets bad.

I have to lean on God,
    I have to hold up my rod.

Cries of the Soul

The enemy hates what Gods given me,
    I have to fight him you see.

Glory to God, praise be to Him today,
    for taking me back and washing my sins away.

LOVE IS. . . .

Love is precious, love is kind,
    love is real hard to find.

If you come across love, in life,
    hold it close, make it your wife.

Love is forgiveness, love is letting go,
    love is you and me as a whole.

Love is beautiful, like a rose,
    it doesn't lie, it doesn't pose.

Love looks after, love protects,
    love doesn't envy, it doesn't wreck.

Love is honest, love is pure,
    love is gentle, it endures.

Love is caring, love trusts,
    love doesn't fight, it doesn't fuss.

Love isn't jealous, it doesn't lust,
    love is true when it's just us.

Love is compromise, love preserves,
    love is what you deserve.

I love you so very much,
    and treasure your precious touch.

Cries of the Soul

Love is forever, it never fails,
    love is strong, it prevails.

Love doesn't go away, it doesn't leave,
    it's always here; ready to receive.

This is what love is to me,
    this is how it should be.

I love you more than you'll ever know,
    more than I could ever show.

God's blessing on us, He gave us love,
    sent straight from above.

Hold on and don't let go of us
    just accept that we are one from God's trust.

Love

    Is

        Us

                Always

                    Has

                      Been

                          Always

                              Will

                                  Be

"God's Hand"

As I Awoke,
    He canceled the yoke.

God waved His hand,
    the demons listen, when He commands.

God's hand touched me,
    He healed me and set me free.

As I Awoke,
    the chains were broke.

My life was healed,
    In an instant, His power was sealed.

He gave me everything back,
    for nothing I would lack.

As I Awoke,

My prayer He heard,
    the angels sang like birds.

Rejoice and be glad,
    He took away all the bad.

Praise His Holy Name,
    because He healed the shame.

Cries of the Soul

As I Awoke,

God did a new thing,
    grace and favor He did bring.

I obeyed His laws,
    and He fixed my flaws.

I served Him and love His perfect plan,
    praise to be God for His hand.

I Am New

My old life was one of destruction,
    the Devil made sure; I couldn't function.

When it rained it poured,
    the Devil cut me up with his sword.

Going lower than I've ever gone,
    God sang a new song.

He reached down and took hold of me,
    a new creature He formed me to be.

God's promises; they are all truth and both beauty,
    because it's His duty.

He renewed my soul to rest,
    and healed my heart; to it's best.

God made me new,
    set me free and in Him I grew.

True joy He restored to me,
    I'm happy with the me, I've turned out to be.

He does new things with a new creature,
    tune into His great feature.

Fly like a bird, open your wings,
    soar to everlasting life, as the angels sing.

Cries of the Soul

Just ask God; God make me new,
    make me your very few.

He will touch you right where you are,
    your prayers, don't travel far.

He is here to listen to you,
    and will carry you through.

Cries of the Soul

"Enemy No – More"

The enemy comes and tries to knock me off course,
    but God comes to save me, riding on His white horse.

The enemy plots and schemes against me,
    but God gives me tools to fight, cause He's on my team.

The enemy has no control,
    he sets a trap, but I step right over the hole.

God equips me with strength and power,
    and the enemy is left feeling sour.

The enemy tempts,
    as I praise and repent.

The enemy cannot deliver me out of God's hand,
    because I have weapons from the mighty man.

The enemy can only do what I allow,
    you ask how?

The enemy can get your thoughts by uttering lies,
    fear and anxiety can arise.

But God gave us the truth through His Word,
    hold fast to it; its life, keep what you heard.

Cries of the Soul

Don't let the enemy get in your head,
    God promises blessings, prosperity and peace; if you listen
    to what He said.

Follow the Lord,
    fight Satan with your sword.

Throw him out as fast as he came,
    cast him back to his fiery flame.

FORGIVENESS

I have done a lot of things in my life,
    that have caused agony and strife.

The anger and the pain,
    is too deep to begin to explain.

It started at a very young age,
    it turned from hurt to rage.

Drugs took this all away,
    but God found me on a special day.

He forgave me for it all,
    now I don't have to fall.

Jesus died a painful death for me,
    He's opened my eyes, now I can see.

From happiness to joy He delivered me,
    because of Him, I can be what He created me to be.

Thankful is what I am,
    because of the blood of the Lamb.

The Devil had me in his hand,
    but now through grace, I'm in God's land.

Cries of the Soul

I am not scared, I do not fear,
    because He comforts me and wipes my tear.

He's giving me back what the Devil took,
    because He forgives, it cannot be shook.

Thank you God for all your love,
    and your hand that protects from above.

"Fear"

Fear is not from me,
    it is from my enemy.

He is a liar, he does deceive,
    have faith in Me and receive.

A few things I want you to know,
    trust in Me, not your foe.

Stand up and be strong,
    through Me, you can never go wrong.

Look in the basket and get your fruit,
    I planted the seed, powerful is the root.

As it matures and grows,
    wait for it, for it comes as the wind blows.

Your purpose is special, it belongs to you,
    I blessed you with talents, to do the work you do.

The devil will come in from time to time,
    to do his evil, much like a crime.

He's here to stop what I start,
    but take my wisdom and be smart.

Cries of the Soul

He can only do what you allow,
    stomp on him and take a bow.

I defeated him, so can you.

Don't let him give you fear,
    open your ears and hear.

My voice; my shepherd listen,
    through the wind it glistens.

Fear not my child,
    his (the enemy) schemes are wild.

He is here to kill, steal and destroy,
    lean on My Word, it holds the key.

To every secret my story

And in it is my complete will,
    obey and all your desires I will fulfill.

Joy and peace be with you today,
    now go to others and say;
    Jesus is the only way.

"No Trust In Men"

They give you advice,
    and maybe it will suffice.

They tell you this, they tell you that,
    but there as smart as a rat.

They don't believe in me, or my word,
    deceived by the enemy, in everything they heard.

Immorality the words they pass to you,
    I come to tell you it isn't true.

Find peace In me, follow my word,
    It's sweet and precious; like a little bird.

Psalms and Proverbs are moral & complete,
    through my instructions, you will defeat.

Matthew, Mark, Luke & John,
    obey and you can't go wrong.

It's clear for all to see,
    promises & blessings to set you free.

Why then do you take earthly advice,
    they don't know, it's like rolling the dice

Cries of the Soul

Lean not on your own understanding,
    but trust and believe it is outstanding.

Follow me and have faith in my ways,
    and joy & happiness will follow your days.

Trust not men,
    they live in sin.

Trust in Jesus, my son,
    the battle he has won.

I Love My Children

My children I sit on a rock,
    through prayer, I will protect the whole flock.

Obey me and follow my ways,
    and I will comfort you, all of your days.

I will carry you through the fire,
    I will give you all your hearts desire.

Worship and honor me,
    and my spirit will lead you, to who I formed you to be.

My love for you is so great,
    your destiny awaits.

I know you, and I know your heart,
    never again will my mercy part.

I detest evil, and hate lying lips,
    they never have enough from your they rip.

But I have come to heal,
    and even through the devil has to kill.

I restore my children's dreams.

Glorify me,
    and I will give you victory.

Cries of the Soul

Sit on my rock and rest,
    for you, will have the best.

Wait on me, through the rain,
    and your enemies will perish in vein.

I hear your cries, and feel your pain,
    but do not drive yourself insane.

Your day is coming when you will be free,
    your miracle awaits, and joy you will see.

Praise my name,
    and your enemies will be put to shame.

For your broken heart will soon depart,
    and your new life will start.

FALLING

When you fall take hold,
    of the lord's hand and be bold.

There never was success without weight,
    we learn, we live, were never late.

There's a lesson in every fall,
    for to be perfected we must stand tall.

In mistakes we stretch and learn turn,
    to know which way to turn.

Sometimes we need to trip,
    to release the enemies grip.

The practice gets us ready,
    for one day we will be steady.

To fail is to succeed,
    for the others we will feed.

Be strong in the lord,
    let him accomplish concord.

Don't give up you day is coming,
    when the enemy will take off running.

Cries of the Soul

Your in preparation for something great,
    and soon you will meet your divine fate.

Don't be scared or overwhelmed.

PURPOSE

God has a will and purpose for me,
    in the pain it's hard to see.

They say to have faith,
    to fight the good fight, to win the race.

The vision seems so clear,
    but I see the opposite when I look in the mirror.

The enemy comes in with doubt –n-fear,
    then I hear god say look up here.

He tells me I'm doing right,
    that's why I'm in this fight.

The enemy is opposing, for your purpose is good,
    get through another day is what I understood.

There's many bumps along this path,
    but there's vengeance in his wrath.

In due season I will win,
    when his glory begins.

There is a purpose for this all,
    for every step I fall.

Cries of the Soul

But by getting up I succeed,
    he brings harvest with every seed.

With every sacrifice I give,
    there's another reason to live.

God see's beginning to end,
    every struggle, every rend.

There is a purpose in the pain,
    there is justice in the rain.

My testimony for all to hear,
    shows my strength in the fear.

My endurance in my troubles,
    and the joy I found in the rubble.

You see there is a purpose to this,
    so don't give up, don't miss.

For God will give you double in the end,
    for being faithful as his friend.

He has a purpose bigger than you know,
    to do so much more and to help you grow.

It's the Darkest Before Dawn

It's the darkest before the dawn,
    satan uses me for his pawn.

He attacks night and day,
    to take your destiny away.

If it's raining really hard,
    and your life feels marred.

If trouble comes down like a flood,
    trust in god and lean on the blood.

Because it's nothing you have done wrong,
    it's because god is singing your life song.

It is big; it is grand,
    so get up and take a stand.

Fight the good fight,
    with his power and might.

He will not leave you nor let you down,
    he will take you to the next round.

Be persistent; don't give up in the battle,
    for god's coming through with a victory shatter.

Cries of the Soul

It will all be worth it in the end,
    rely on him he will defend.

He is your strong tower,
    the one who give you your power.

So hold up your shield,
    and do not yield.

But stand firm in all of this,
    and the reward will be bliss.

He sees your hardship; he sees your pain,
    all of this is not in vein.

He will bring you through,
    so believe in him in all you do.

A double portion is on it's way to you,
    all his promises are true.

It may be dark in this season,
    but there is a good reason.

"It's The Darkest Before the Dawn"

CRY IN TROUBLE

I'm in trouble hear my cry,
   "O" me "O" my.

This affliction is hard to bare,
   I'm so empty, this isn't fair.

"O" Lord save me,
   from my vast enemy.

Who seeks my ruin all day long,
   somehow this has to be wrong.

Deliver me from this pain,
   bring your peace to your ordained.

Show your face in this storm,
   I'm weak and worn.

Lift me up with your right hand,
   bring me into the promise land.

Let your joy be my strength,
   for this is hard and long in length.

Help me see the good in this fight,
   take vengeance lord and make it right.

Cries of the Soul

Bring your comfort as you hold me,
    through the night protect and set me free.

Cries of the Soul

VOLUME TWO

SON

My dear son,
 This battle is about won.

I pray for you day and night,
 because today I send you light.

I pray you receive,
 I pray you believe.

In the dreams of your heart,
 that you could see my love; that shines for you; my art.

"O" how I long to see your face,
 to show you my loves embrace.

You are always on my mind,
 I'm sorry Seth for the hurt you find.

I wish things were different for you son,
 I pray healing would be complete and done.

Cries of the Soul

I hope today you can sense my thought,
    of my hurting heart; as you are sought.

I never forgot about my sweet boy,
    may your heart be filled with joy.

I want you to know,
    a mothers love; can only grow.

So as you go about your day,
    I just want to say;

I'm sorry for your pain,
    I didn't mean to leave you in the rain.

I wish I could take it all away,
    and I will someday.

Every tear you have cried,
    will soon be dried.

On the day,
    the sun comes out to play.

And until then,
    pray to God; He will defend.

Lift your head,
    kneel beside your bed.

God is there,
    give it to Him, cast your care.

Miracles do take place.

MY JESS

My dear Jess,
    the day I saw you I became blessed.

A princess wrapped in a blanket; I stare
    this beauty has to be rare.

I remember the good old days,
    nothing is a haze.

I ran across you photo today,
    such a beautiful sight I must say.

I miss you Jess,
    so much my heart can't rest.

Your eyes;
    remind me of the stars in the skies.

I want to hold you so bad,
    at times I became sad.

Cries of the Soul

I pray to God at four,
    He said have faith, I restore.

I believe I will see you again,
    know I love you Jess; until then.

EMILY

My dear Daughter Emily I love you,
    you're the cause of what I do.

My heart was broken,
    when those words were spoken.

When I gave birth:
    and had to leave you behind,
    the pain so strong; it made me blind.

You were taken against my will,
    hurt is all I feel.

I never forgot you,
    my little Rose that's Who?

You are so special to me:
    Your beauty sustains,
    as tears embrace the pains.

Cries of the Soul

You don't know who I am,
    but I'm your momma mam.

One day I will see you again,
    and a relationship will begin.

Until that day comes my Daughter,
    know my love grows hotter.

You are the apple of my eye,
    it hurt so deep, when I had to say good bye.

LOVING ZACK

I once carried a little boy,
    who brought my laughter and joy.

A closeness so rare,
    separate us if you dare.

He never wanted to leave my side,
    his love for me could never divide.

A glimpse at him now,
    I just say wow.

He's getting so big and tall,
    this pain tops them all.

Zack your mommies boy,
    forever you will be my joy.

The pictures of us tell the story:
    of love and life,
        one I had close, through the strife.

Cries of the Soul

I never forgot you my dear son,
    if anything you're the reason I don't run.

The reason I have started anew,
    a deep love I possess for you.

So as you grow and learn,
    know mommy's love is stern.

You're in my heart,
    and that will never part.

BAY

My little boy,
    what a blessing you are today.

You're the child, who started my turn around,
    you're the reason the Lord found;

My heart just in time,
    a gift from Heaven, your all mine.

More precious than gold,
    to see this miracle unfold.

The glowing on your face,
    helps me remember every trace;
    as this life we embrace.

There's a purpose here,
    for you dear.

So remember this,
    Jesus made a beautiful bliss.

Cries of the Soul

He made us for each other,
    so His love could cover.

His ways are all knowing,
    so remember this as your growing.

Seeds

Proverbs 18:21

A seed planted is a seed sown,
    and in the soil it is grown.

What seeds are you planting,
    what words are you chanting.

Is it life or is it death,
    is it destruction or is it breath.

Is it hard or is it light,
    Is it wrong or is it right.

Whatever you plant will be rooted,
    and the other will be booted.

Are you singing or are you growing,
    are you praising or are you moaning.

It's your decision, you get to decide,
    will you abide or divide.

Cries of the Soul

It's your seed to do as you will,
    it's your day, do you want to hurt or heal.

It's your fruit,
    it's your root.

It's your heart, it's your passion,
    it's your action.

Eating your fruit is assured,
    what will be your next word?

Think it, speak it and live it today,
    your words have power in every way.

VISION
(Proverbs 29:18)

I used to be a woman with no vision,
    running in cycles of collision.

I used to be a woman with no dreams,
    my days were countless beams.

I used to be a woman with no light,
    my life immersed me with blind sight.

Troubled with regret and fear,
    I seen emptiness in the mirror.

Anger and hate in the depths of my soul,
    burning black as coal.

A wounded spirit shattered and spoken the pieces of me
    lying in ruin,
    nothing left I was shun.

Cries of the Soul

God seen me and showed me His grace,
    through the trail a light was the trace.

He slowly cut away my darkened heart,
    I found a love so supreme, I couldn't depart.

Surrounded by His amazing ways,
    I found myself with vision in my days.

So sharp and full of passion,
    He gave me a cup full of ration.

My vision is so clear,
    I see beauty as I look in the mirror.

A story to tell,
    He opened up the deep well.

He touched me with all His majesty,
    He emanated me with a kiss of reality.

He gave me a heart of wonders,
    my broken spirit became asunder.

I'm full of vision,
    for my calling, I have risen.

From ashes to beauty,
    serving the Lord is my delight and duty.

POWER
Ephesians 1:17

There's power on high,
    as God works His Spirit draws nigh.

Put all your not into Him,
    as darkness breaks in.

You are weak but He is strong,
    this battle it seems so long.

But don't give up in the storm,
    because it's here your strength is born.

Trust and rely in His power,
    to do a work in this hour.

It hurts but it's a must,
    don't get discouraged or distrust.

But know He brought you here,
    to heal you of all fear.

Cries of the Soul

Be strong in the Lord,
    pick up your sword.

There's power in His Name,
    So awake your soul and remain,

patient, Steadfast and hold still,
    as wisdom is His reveal.

You will come out better than before,
    So don't hide, walk through the door.

Pick up your faith,
    without any haste.

Be humble before God,
    and He will smite the enemy with His rod.

He will show himself strong in this,
    instead of shame you will get bliss.

Let Him form your glorious fruit,
    and do not argue or dispute.

He is God, He is great,
    stand up and meet your fate.

This is you – walking,
    straight into breakthrough.

YOUR WAY OR MINE
Isaiah 30:21

I heard a voice,
    telling me to make a choice.

Blessed is he who waits on the Lord,
    woe to him who's flesh is adored.

My own path,
    strangled out by His wrath.

My heart grew cold,
    as trouble seemed to unfold.

I heard a voice,
    say follow me and rejoice.

I turned around and began again,
    towards the path where God sustains.

I cried and wept for days,
    as the Lord molded my ways.

Cries of the Soul

I smiled – I laughed,
    I uprooted the task.

I found joy and I found peace,
    as pride began to cease.

I learned one thing sure,
    The Lords way is pure.

Trusting in myself,
    means lack of wealth.

There is a way to get your dreams,
    but trust God with the puppet strings.

He knows what and when,
    and how to perfectly defend.

Lean on God with all your heart,
    He will mend the pieces and newness will start.

Without God I am nothing,
    but with Him I am something.

Cries of the Soul

SINFUL CHURCH
Isaiah 42

Why are we yelling,
   why are we rebelling.

All this hate among His people,
   all this sin in His steeple.

No wonder the Body isn't reaching,
   no wonder there's no healing in his teaching.

The Church today has lost its praise,
   its lost its heart in these last days.

It worships itself for gain,
   it pushes away the ordained.

It's jealous and its full of pride,
   it's on the devil's side.

Who are we representing in this hour,
   is your Church dead or full of power.

Cries of the Soul

Are there miracles flowing,
    or just vainness words blowing.

The Word says to heal the sick and raise the dead,
    The Body has forgotten the Godhead.

Its lifted itself to a mantle of praise,
    where is God through the haze.

There is no anointing, there is no fire,
    just bondage, bidding satan's conspire.

The Word says, do as I do,
    and even greater things you shall do.

Miracles, signs and wonders,
    are you in an all-time plunder?

We are not healing with the power,
    the Church has went sour.

People in wheelchairs should walk,
    the deaf should talk.

The Glory should be so thick,
    we should be knocked over with a heavy brick.

God's looking for people with a heart so pure,
    so He can lead and stir.

Stir up the gifts of the spirit,
    God is talking can you hear it?

Come forward if you will,
    let the Lord come and heal.

HEAVEN

Is Heaven for real?
   is happiness all I will feel?

Are the streets really gold?
   are the walls really sapphire and jasper That's that I wastold!!!

I can only imagine how great,
   what a beautiful fate.

Being with Jesus, bowing at His feet,
   feeling His heartbeat.

Being in His glorious light,
   seeing eyes of fire of power and might.

What a day this will be,
   what a sight, I can't wait to see.

To eat at His table and drink His wine,
   I am His and He is mine.

Cries of the Soul

I can only imagine riding on the clouds,
    hearing the angels singing loud.

The music so sound,
    where true joy is found.

One day I will go home to God,
    I will be awed.

From beauty and simplicity of the gates,
    my crown awaits.

I will live for the Lord in all I do,
    and I pray you will to.

PROMISE

My heart is broke,
    for my past is my yoke.

Victory seems do far away,
    how do I get past the pain of today?

I have promises from God held inside,
    this trouble won't subside.

It all seems like a long ride,
    in the waves of a tide.

Delay after delay,
    as once again another day passes away.

Life is passing me up,
    there's tears in my cup.

His promises are so great,
    but all I do is sit here and wait.

Cries of the Soul

I think about the every word,
    the promises I heard.

Where are they,
    as I walk in hope today,
    maybe tomorrow's the day.

LIVING BREAD

Jesus is the living bread,
    go to Him to get fed.

He promises a fresh filling,
    and His love is the sealing.

He gave up His life, in the flesh,
    He gave us peace and rest.

His flesh is true food and drink,
    to get to God, He's the only link.

His promises I shall thirst no more,
    for the stripes; His body tore.

Have faith and trust,
    because He is fair and just.

He who believes has eternal life,
    Heaven's Bread makes us ripe

Cries of the Soul

Eat it and never die,
    Drink it and your wells will never dry.

I ate and abundance flowed,
    I drank and broke the mold.

What a price to pay,
    to give me life I have today.

THOUGHTS OF THE WORD

Sitting here looking out the window,
    seeing the souls in the shadows.

Who knows not the Lord,
    Hell is the concord.

Seeing and feeling God's pain,
    for a hurting world living in vein.

They don't even know,
    their destruction, when the trumpets blow.

They lack wisdom, knowledge & understanding,
    what's left when God comes landing.

For some it will be a happy day,
    but for lost souls, the fire won't delay.

Torture forever,
    and it will never sever.

Cries of the Soul

I'm thinking about the world today,
    why would a God do sinners this way.

But why would sinners walk away,
    it's my choice to put embers in the wood.

For me I choose life and love,
    I choose God who is healer from above.

Cries of the Soul

BROKEN

Not that long ago,
    I was in a pit and death was the flow.

I'm sitting here today,
    wondering how I got away.

One touch of His Glory,
    now I live to tell my story.

The flames of Hell surrounded me,
    but God came down and broke the chains of bondage
    and set me free.

My past is a path,
    but God too wrath.

He found me on that dark road,
    carrying a heavy load.

The Holy Spirit saw my need,
    came in and gave me my feed.

Cries of the Soul

Crack cocaine was my life,
    inside me was agony and strife.

A woman inside,
    trying to hide.

A broken spirit of many wounds tore to the core,
    inside me was a war.

I didn't care if I lived or died,
    I was so tired of the lies.

The devil ripped my heart into two,
    I just didn't know what to do.

I had nothing left,
    I was a victim of the enemy's theft.

He stole everything from me,
    but one day the Glory made me see.

My soul was awake,
    in the Heavens there was a break.

My purpose here on Earth,
    is to bring many to a new birth.

You can't be too low to be found,
    He will reach down to the ground.

It's never to late,
    to come to Heaven's gate.

Healing and restoration is here,
    open your heart and let Jesus appear.

Cries of the Soul

He's all around knocking on the door,
    you are His child that He bore.

Wake up and see,
    there's a better life for you and me.

AMAZING GRACE

Amazing grace,
    O' how the Lord embraced.

How sweet the sound,
    the day I was found.

That saved a wretch like me,
    for the devil's playground I couldn't see.

I once was lost,
    but Jesus paid the cost.

Now I'm found,
    I'm a rising army against the blood hound.

I was blind,
    but now I'm filled with wine.

Now I can see,
    what's standing in front of me.

Twas grace that that taught my heart to fear,
    power surged my ears to hear.

Twas grace my fears relieved,
    as the word I believed.

How precious did that grace appear,
    as my beacon was the steer.

The hour I first believed,
    as healing manifested as my reprieve.

Amazing grace,
    it happened as God embraced.

A Heart for Jesus

The cross is to be,
    the grounds of you and me.

To understand His Flesh,
    was torn; made into a bloody mess.

He was beaten black and blue,
    so we could step through.

The nothing and cutting,
    as His disciples came turning.

He died piercing, agonizing pain,
    but not in vain.

How beautiful the blood,
    that was the holy lands flood.

Running out in streams of rivers
    as Jesus grew cold and shivered.

Cries of the Soul

As people spit on Him and laughed,
    He looked up and said Father cancel – your wrath.

Have mercy as I die in there place,
    love them and hive them grace.

The Kingdom of Heaven is near,
    lift up your hands, worship in fear.

The Lord God Almighty in awe,
    to your knees: fall.

For He died,
    so we could forever be tied.

So we could be as one,
    so once and for all it could be done.

That blood that was shed,
    so our souls could be fed.

So we could live and rest,
    He gave His very best.

So today don't think lightly,
    of the Lord Almighty.

A horrible death,
    as He took His last breath.

So this world He could save,
    as He rose from the grave.

He carried it all away,
    on that Glorious Day.

Cries of the Soul

So today as you embrace the cross,
    remember the blood loss.

As you go about blessed in your day,
    say thank you Jesus in every way.

THE ENEMIES LIES

I heard the enemy whisper in my ear,
    believe my lies and be filled with fear.

He said doubt the Word,
    he came to take the news you heard.

The truth will set you free,
    believe my lies he decrees.

He doesn't want to let you go,
    he liked you depressed and low.

He knows God restores and heals,
    don't listen to the accuser for he steals.

Everything good in your path,
    but fight him and break his staff.

Tell him he is a liar,
    and he wants to steal your fire.

Cries of the Soul

Tell him get under your feet,
    tell him to retreat.

Strike him with faith,
    smite him leaving no trace.

Kill the whole Army in the camp,
    shine God's Lamp.

Show him the exit door,
    tell him no more.

I know who I am in Christ,
    and to take a hike.

You are an overcomer, you can win,
    surrender to God, say no to sin.

Don't give him a foothold,
    but be violent and bold.

The devil is a liar and a thief,
    defeat him with joy as your sheaf.

Lift your hands up to God,
    He is your strength, He is your rod.

THE ANSWER

The weeping tears from my eyes,
    as I look into the blue skies.

O' how looking into them sifts things,
    O' the feeling it brings.

There's something about looking up,
    it's filling; as water to a cup.

It says, He is lifter of my head,
    that's the verse I just read.

So as you go on your journey today,
    confess loudly and say:

Lord you are on my shield,
    you're the Glory in my field.

You are the one who lifts my head,
    you Lord give me my daily bread.

Cries of the Soul

As I say this as my shield,
    the Spirit in my atmosphere builds.

A covenant between God and me,
    the peace floods in like a raging sea.

This is how I change,
    the heart and mind range.

Breaking Free

The serpent couldn't sting me anymore,
    my house was firm, from the fight it bore.

So He began anew,
    something He knew.

He used my family, yes it's true,
    We don't wrestle against flesh and blood – for he is
    ruthless, there's no end to what he'll do.

This fight goes on and on inside,
    learning is the key to finish the ride.

Experience is the way to win,
    for through failure, I find my best friend.

Jesus comes to me to save,
    to make me bold and brave.

I will get up and fight again,
    to fight this fight of righteousness vs. sin.

Cries of the Soul

What matters is how you finish,
    because He's there to replenish.

Stand up tall and remember he won,
    He died and rose, then it was done.

If He can do it, so can we,
    so rise up Child of God as the chains fall and you are set free.

CASTING OFF

The assignment was broken,
    by declarations spoken.

The enemy has to flee,
    from the curse he put on me.

Speak and cancel the deep array,
    break the heaviness of the day.

What I speak must come to pass,
    I bind the wasters of hidden brass.

I smite my enemy, in my path,
    God may you have vengeance and wrath.

I bind and loose that here on Earth,
    I renounce my sin and declare new birth.

I surrenders to a God that's so good,
    even though He's not understood.

Cries of the Soul

His ways are best;
    He keeps me hidden in the crest.

It's not always easy to obey,
    but listen if you may.

Your way has got you nowhere fast,
    give it to Him as your cares are cast.

"Transition"

The enemy had me for so long,
    every years something else went wrong.

He wounded my soul,
    his works took a toll.

I believed as he spoke,
    destruction was here as I awoke.

He said do it so I did,
    I was his to bid.

A puppet on a string,
    terror he would bring.

The evil around me was in control,
    it had me trapped in a hole.

The strangeness of the dark,
    I was craving just one little spark.

Cries of the Soul

As Jesus drew close,
    I experienced love in a little dose.

The light came in and shined so bright,
    I was pierced with beauty and sight.

Oh how He saves,
    I am now strong and brave.

Thank you Jesus for showing me the way,
    for the truth in the words You say.

The devil is a liar,
    he had me in the much and the mire.

But no more; the truth set me free,
    and He'll do this for you, as He did for me.

Cries of the Soul

I'M A NEW ME

I can hear the devil whisper in my ear,
    yes his lies I can hear.

I can feel his evil presence all around,
    as the pressure of attack is abound.

The enticement of all my past sins,
    but tonight that spirit won't win.

A heart of stone has been healed,
    a new person has been revealed.

I can tell him no and feel good,
    because newness is understood.

Old things have passed away,
    new things I declare for this day.

I don't want to di those things,
    I want the joy the Lord brings.

Cries of the Soul

I thought I had to be strong enough to win,
    but changed heart is victory over sin.

He will never give up on me,
    attacking me is all he can see.

But I refuse,
    I will not lose.

I stand up and fight,
    this war with my fists held tight.

Devil I give you no more of my heart,
    I command you go; that you depart.

Never again will I be chained,
    never again will I be shamed.

Jesus has wiped me clean as snow,
    He picked me up where you left me low – I found it ,
    I'll never let go.

The love I never knew,
    for this love I say I do.

I've been touched by God's hand,
    in His arms I ran.

So today I confess,
    instead of curses I'm blessed.

My Heart

A beating heart pumping blood to veins alive in the flesh,
    dead in the rest.

My eyes can no longer open,
    the tears, no more words spoken.

I reach for a breath,
    all I feel is death.

My bones are soft,
    the pain of agony and loss.

I feel empty & hard,
    my soul is hurt and mared.

Now I'm a light in this world,
    sent into love twirled.

The secrets kept inside,
    His spirit I abide.

Cries of the Soul

The matter,
    as every hurt shatters.

He turned it all around,
    I am no longer bound.

There is life; in His tree,
    He wipes away the debris.

Who am I, I do not know, I'm a girl,
    sent to dance & whirl.

To speak,
    to the hurting & the weak.

To comfort & console,
    to shed light into that black hole.

To be a healer, on a broken road,
    to lighten the load.

To give a hope and a caring hand,
    to make salvation your land.

Look up into the sky,
    it's Jesus passing by.

It's Him you just met,
    it's your son He set.

He holds you in His heart,
    so go ahead make a fresh start.

Go into the arms of Jesus....

MY PAST MADE ME

So much of my life displaced,
    the enemy is who I stare in the face.

He has taken so much from me,
    this road; where has it led me to see.

I thank God for this broken road,
    it has made me the woman inside, unfold.

My past took me out with a blast,
    but today it's made me who I am; bold and strong as brass.

I am who I am because,
    of who I was.

Today as I look back,
    I don't see regret and lack.

Cries of the Soul

I see a woman full of glory,
    with a beautiful story.

I've lived and I've failed,
    but I've swam and sailed.

My story is unique,
    it is no longer bleak.

He experienced and I've learned,
    and today I yearn; for His Fire to burn.

It's Him I can't live without,
    It's Him I live to tell about.

TODAY'S WORLD

There's so much going on around me,
    in the Heavenlies where I can't see.

Devils and demons,
    taking captive the regions.

This world is fading,
    full of people hating.

Where is God in all of this,
    as the world takes its shift.

They threw God out,
    so no wonder violence is all you hear about.

He can't come to save,
    when evil is what the world craves.

America got what it wanted,
    in all its growth stunted.

Cries of the Soul

Where in all this debate,
    when we're lying in our own fate.

We chose to live this way,
    so what is there to say.

Turn back to Him,
    or this world will remain dim.

It's your choice,
    America where's your voice.

Quit doing wrong,
    and stand up strong.

Realizes the error of your ways,
    and God will bless your days.

But if you keep evil in your heart,
    mass destruction will not part.

What are we to say in the news,
    do you not see the clues.

Of prophecy coming alive,
    disobedience in on the arise.

For He's not a liar, has He said,
    it's in the Bible written in red.

So next time something appears,
    know it's lack of fear.

Go ahead fight against the Lord,
    but beware of His sword.

GIANTS

There's giants in the land,
    your defeat they demand.

You must kill;
    before they steal.

There the destiny giants,
    come to make you defiant.

To entangle you in a trap of defeat,
    to chain your feet.

Be persistent; don't give in,
    victory is about to begin.

Right at the finish line,
    your light will shine.

To break forth the dawn,
    no longer satan's pawn.

Cries of the Soul

He loses; you win,
    as you say goodbye to sin.

Spell out his defeat,
    as his powers you unseat.

GOD'S POWER

There's secrets to having His power,
    it's in drawing near to His tower.

The more I die, the more He lives,
    the story is in the piercing of His ribs.

I follow Him in all His footsteps,
    through the valley to the mountain depths.

I can have spiritual blessing,
    in Him I am resting.

But every pain He suffered and endured,
    is pain on me that's emerged.

It's the way I must serve, so I can save and heal,
    so I can make my appeal.

The thorns on His head,
    remember the blood shed.

Cries of the Soul

That's power and I must do it to,
    to accomplish what I was sent to do.

His life is a reflection of mine,
    the goodness and the sadness combined.

Thank you Jesus for all you've done,
    thank you for the war you've won.

You are more precious to me,
    than anyone could ever be.

No matter what I sit beside you,
    no matter what I go through.

I love you Lord,
    with you I'm a concord.

You are my life and my love,
    thank you for the power from above.

HIS PRESENCE

In the stillness of His Presence,
   I am soaked and rinsed.

In the quiet I am restored,
   as I praise and worship the Lord.

I am hungry and thirsty for Him,
   through the haze of my withered limb.

As sin is cast out,
   I'm filled with the fire they talk about.

Everyday my heart gets closer, I find;
   the presence from behind.

A touch from Heaven; I felt
   as my spirit; it melts.

The Glory I have found,
   in the stillness of no sound.

Cries of the Soul

Laying in the quietness; soaking,
    marinating and invoking.

New levels of water spring forth,
    as He prepares me for my course.

I am a daughter of the Most High,
    He shows up the moment I die.

And as I seek His face,
    I see His plan for my race.

I have been chosen in this hour,
    to do His will and be filled with power.

THE DESERT

The desert is lonely and cold,
    but it's here God molds.

It's full of pain,
    but it's here you remain.

The scenery is dull,
    this place is push and pull.

Being pulled to the left, then the right,
    the tears are my only fight.

Living and learning,
    walking and discerning.

I'm in a training,
    there's a reason it's raining.

I'm waiting on the sun,
    but it won't come till I'm done.

Cries of the Soul

God is shaping this vessel,
    it will happen, no matter the wrestle.

The more I say no, the more He carves,
    He won't leave me to starve.

He's peeling back all the seeds,
    the pain, is so intense it bleeds.

Soon I will be a perfected art,
    and my destiny will start.

I am to be used,
    then in His Spirit I will infuse.

It isn't easy dying to myself,
    but soon He'll take me off the shelf.

He uses bad for good and when the test you have stood,
    abundant life is what's understood.

THE DAYS IN A WEEK
Genesis 1:1-31

There's seven days in a week,
    God's Earth was dark and bleak.

On the first day, He created light,
    He made the Earth beautiful and bright.

On the second day, He made water and sky,
    and was very pleased by the sight of His eye.

On the third day, He created plants and dry ground,
    the beauty of life was found.

On the fourth day, He created the sun, moon and stars;
    amazed and delighted at what He did do far.

On the fifth day, He made sea creatures and bird
    of every kind, tribe and herd.

On the sixth day He made Adam and Eve,
    covered them and promised to never leave.

Cries of the Soul

They were the apple of His eye,
    He was pleased and heard every cry.

On the seventh day, He rested as He looked over
    everything He made,
    and smiled for it was good He portrayed.

He gave man authority over all the Earth,
    but satan came and that was rebirthed.

We gave Him our keys,
    as we fell to our knees.

But Jesus died,
    so we took it back because satan lied.

So today wake up as he reveals,
    not to take the devils deals.

No longer will he steal,
    no longer will he kill.

We have the power
    so turn your ashes into beauty this hour.

Eat the giants as your bread,
    pay attention to what Jesus said.

I give you the power to bind and loose,
    the authority over his abuse.

So put him in his place,
    as you seek God's face.

The truth will set you free,
    victory is what we see.

Cries of the Soul

KEEPING GOD IN A BOX

Why are we keeping God in a box,
    the things He wants to do is locked.

Doubt and unbelief,
    making our thoughts and listening to the thief.

Listen; if Jesus di it so can we, it's written even greater
    things you shall do,
        so quit reasoning because it's true.

We're denying God and accepting the devil's plea,
    submit and he will flee.

Jesus said to cure the sick, drive out demons and raise the
    dead,
        so why are we shunning; these people need fed.

The Church laughs and scoffs when God is moving,
    when Jesus is what they're proving.

Cries of the Soul

They say it's a colt,
    they wanna bring it to a holt.

My people are <u>affected</u> by lack of knowledge,
    it's written as a hedge.

Jesus is the same yesterday, today and forever,
    so I pray Lord these mindsets sever.

No longer shall you be held back,
    or the Church will lack.

Come to the water,
    and drink from your Heavenly Father.

Open up the river banks,
    come into the high ranks.

Let God move as He wills,
    instead of making Him hold still.

Let offense subside,
    let the Spirit rise.

Let the atmosphere change,
    let Jesus be the range.

Let miracles, signs and wonders
    come like thunder.

Let the Holy Spirit in,
    so a real Church can begin.

Cries of the Soul

THE VOICES

There's a voice I hear,
    does it bring joy or fear?

Is it good or is it bad?
    Does it make me happy or sad?

Jesus is my guide,
    the one in whom I confide.

But I must test the voices,
    so that I can make the right choices.

Your enemy want to guide you in the wrong direction,
    use discretion.

He will come as an angel of light,
    locate the enemy with Heaven's delight.

It is written to test the spirits,
    so don't believe it just because you hear it.

Destiny has a path,
    look at the devil and laugh.

Follow your one true guide,
    let all other voices subside.

Cries of the Soul

GENERATION

Today's generation what have we become,
   disgraceful things; makes my heart numb.

You see it all around,
   It's an abomination, yet it's found.

We fight for its rights,
   darkness why is it so bright.

It's not normal like people say,
   it's evil lurking in this last day.

Today's generation, what have we become,
   we see it and run.

We turn our head,
   at everything said.

It's in the news,
   evil sits in the pews.

We don't stand up; we're scared to offend,
    this is the message we send.

This hurting world is in trouble,
    entangled in the rubble.

It's written the truth will set you free,
    So people brush back the debris.

Today's generation what an immoral state,
    all this debate.

Has God not said,
    without Him we're dead.

We are on a downslope,
    to a place of no hope.

We need to pray,
    instead of push God away.

Stubbornness and rebellion is at an all-time high,
    witchcraft is passing by.

The evil we're accepting,
    it's our youth it's affecting.

From one generation to the next,
    it's a curse, it is a hex.

Disobedience and seeking our own,
    it's the reason we moan.

People take a hard look,
    at the messages in this book.

Cries of the Soul

Wake up and take off the veil,
    yes your soul is for sale.

God bought it on the cross,
    but we don't care about His loss.

He is still scoffed at today,
    so listen if you may.

Lay it all down,
    to Jesus; thorns of crown.

Rebellion is cursing our days,
    generation, turn back repent of your ways.

SET ME ON FIRE

Set my soul on fire,
    give me my heart's desire.

Pour out your Spirit upon my flesh,
    I want to wear you as a vest.

I'm craving you more and more,
    as I seek you open the door.

I'm seeking something I can't contain,
    something tangible; something real, where I'll never be the same.

Put your power deep within,
    out of control I want to spin.

I'm seeking fresh wine,
    be My strength; be My vine.

I want Heaven here with me,
    your all I wanna see.

Cries of the Soul

Set my soul on fire,
    Your all my desire.

Open up a deep well,
    so people will quit going to hell.

Come through,
    in a mighty way, in what you do.

Fill the earth with your Glory,
    give the miraculous and outstanding story.

Touch the hearts to expect you more,
    for you Lord is whom I adore.

Send your angels to do a job,
    a job, the enemy can't rob.

I want to see you in the signs; a wonder here on Earth,
    fragrance and myrrh.

THE NEW ME

I'm reminded today who I was,
    He never wants me to forget because,

He is the only reason I'm not there,
    me and God make a good pair.

As He choose me for Himself, I choose Him,
    I let Him do the work within.

To wake up and not know who you are,
    to understand you're his star.

I look like I always have on the outside,
    but He took away my pride.

My innocence has been restored,
    I am who I am because of You Lord.

I'm no one, I used to be,
    I am a new me.

Cries of the Soul

All the anger, hate and rage,
    I'm ready to stand on stage.

To tell the world, He is the way,
    change your mind today.

You see my old nature was a pile of sorrow,
    but now today, I have a better tomorrow.

I could never do it without Him,
    He healed my broken limb.

I know where I've been and where I'm going,
    with Him shinning His light; with Him showing.

He leads I follow,
    if I get scared; I take a breath then swallow.

He is all I need,
    He's the only lead.

I love Him with all my heart,
    from His Spirit, I'll never depart.

Thank you Jesus for everything you did,
    thank you I'm no longer hid.

Now I can live to tell,
    how you saved me from hell.

BEAUTIFUL ME

I am a beautiful work of art,
    thought up at the beginning; right from the Lords heart.

He set me aside,
    until it was time for me to reside.

I am one of a kind,
    created by God's Mind.

Precious is everything He made,
    amazed as He marveled and gazed.

I was born at just the right time,
    for history to climb.

To do the things,
    that only God can bring.

I was in His intricate plan,
    all my life is in His hand.

Cries of the Soul

To serve and reverence my master,
    there's nothing more in that box; Alabaster.

The fragrance of my intimacy with Him,
    He gives hope to my tree limb.

I'm everything He created,
    He formed me in my womb.

That's what the Word stated, I'm beautiful and I'm a
    precious stone,
        every part, flesh and bone.

A Dream Seen

In the wisdom of my mind,
    the vision is seen but left behind.

The pictures of the things I desire,
    full of passion; so much fire.

Where do I go from here,
    it hurts not to be near.

I'm locked inside this prison; who has the key,
    to set my heart free.

So much vision; so many dreams,
    such a tragedy it seems.

I do not know where to go,
    or in what direction to flow.

I call upon you Lord of Host,
    the only place my heart can coast.

Cries of the Soul

The rivers and streams,
    carry away my dreams.

No one knows who I am inside,
    this person doesn't wanna hide.

I'm laughed at and looked down upon,
    I sit here and wait on my dawn.

From sun up to sun set, I wait,
    for my destiny for me fate.

To rise and to shine,
    for it all to be mine.

The mystery as it unfolds,
    I release everything I hold.

I'm looking for the key,
    so that I can unlock me.

So I can unlock the chains,
    of everything that sustains.

BATTLE KEYS

Every time I win the battle,
    is a time God has me on a saddle.

Each one I conquer is another wall,
    tore down preventing me from a fall.

Every time I win,
    every time I say no to sin.

It's a wall tore down,
    it's an area no longer bound.

At times it's hard to keep looking ahead,
    but then I see Jesus and hear what He said.

I hear the words of Paul,
    I hear the secret to preventing my fall.

Take hold of what lies ahead, forget what lies behind,
    the past, leave it and beauty you will find.

Cries of the Soul

God has a secret key to every door,
    pray and ask for.

The secrets and Heaven will reveal,
    the answer to every appeal.

DENIED BY HIS PEOPLE

Manifested miracles, signs and wonders,
    God's looking for a people in hunger.

And when He rests His Glory in a place,
    the Church Body scoffs in His face.

They become alarmed and say it's a colt,
    it's the devil and try to bring it to a holt.

The Church is being blinded by the enemies lies,
    they're lifting up satan and letting God pass by.

How is it the devil gets more credit than an all powerful God?
    These miracles manifest at His spoken rod.

And we give praise to the powers of Hell,
    wow; now that's a sight for Christians to tell.

People quit being deceived and accepting that unbelief,
    and stop doubting the High Chief.

Cries of the Soul

He wants to do great things to us today,
    so move out of the way.

If He did it so can we,
    so shut your lips and let it be.

Quit grieving the Holy Spirit,
    open your ears to hear it.

Open your eyes,
    quit letting the Church die.

Quit pushing God away,
    or one day He might say,

I never knew you,
    and this will be true.

Cries of the Soul

DARKNESS
Psalms 23

The deeper I walk, the darker it becomes,
    every road I walk, I succumb.

This path is long and dark,
    I'm searching for just one spark.

Evil is all around me,
    this place – how could it be.

Then I hear God; don't' doubt in the dark what you've
    believed in the light,
    rise up and trust in my might.

A dreary season,
    for a glorious reason.

Like me; you pray for others gain,
    to rescue them from the rain.

Cries of the Soul

As destiny perks,
    evil lurks.

You will make it, stand up tall,
    lean on me and you won't fall.

Be confident and strong,
    and you won't go wrong.

The vision is clear,
    wait for Me to appear.

I'm coming in a dash,
    I'm coming in a flash.

Lift up your eyes,
    God hears your cries.

I'm coming here I am,
    it's God covering you with the blood of the Lamb.

This trial is over; it is at an end,
    no more will He attack, I'm here to defend.

It is written He will come through,
    and His Words are true.

It's your time, it's your season,
    victory is the reason.

You have put him under your feet,
    God returned the cleat.

From this day,
    joy makes the way.

The abundance overflows,
  as God's Glory shows.

Cries of the Soul

YOUR REDEEMER LIVES

I felt the power deep inside,
    like a rushing water tide.

Is this real,
    the electricity I feel.

God's Glory,
    is this part of my story.

For a long time my story has been pain,
    but now the rainbow, now the gain.

Pain always comes first,
    but then the joy comes out to burst.

Wow! What a wonderful power,
    thank you for being my strong tower.

My defender and my hope,
    for not leaving me hanging on that rope.

God is good-God is great,
    He rescued me from being satans bait.

God has never left,
    He released me from the enemy's theft.

All the times I prayed to be free,
    now I know He heard me.

I was captive,
    now joyful I live.

Always know there's a way out,
    so today do a victory shout.

Praise the Lord and do not doubt,
    climb up the mount.

As your climbing remember this,
    every step hurts; but persist.

Joy is on the other side,
    so be strong and abide.

The Lord knows what He has for you,
    it's beautiful; so go all the way through.

Cries of the Soul

THE WORLD WHO NEEDS GOD

My heart is broke,
    for a world in bondage and yoke.

They don't understand or know,
    where they're life is to go.

To wake up and feel this worlds pain,
    of a people living in vein.

That used to be,
    the story in me.

I'd open my eyes,
    and immediately listen to his lies.

I lived for him for so long,
    while my life was so wrong.

Disaster struck,
    it was just my luck.

A hate for this life,
    as satan cheated my strife.

One day the hand of God came to save,
    a small voice said be brave.

He said I'm here,
    give me your fear.

I became aware,
    of this spiritual warfare.

This woman inside,
    a torn life, on a miserable ride.

The reality of God's Being,
    got me to seeing.

A life lived without Him,
    is dark and dim.

We were never intended to be alone,
    to have lifeless bones.

We were meant,
    to come to Him, knees bent.

To lean on His strength and His arms,
    to protect from all harm.

Man has tried to do it His way,
    that's why you're in pain today.

Call out to the God above,
    let Him show you Heaven's love.

PAIN
Psalms 51: 17

A broken and marred vessel,
    crushed and cleated like a pretzel.

Tormented with pain,
    being swallowed by the drain.

Why am I here,
    there's no end, the hurt just switched gear.

I am a door mat,
    they cheer and chat.

They eat me alive,
    from my pain they derive.

My hands so shaky, my muscles so weak,
    my mouth can't speak.

Any words to express how I feel,
    all I know is I wish this wasn't real.

Is it really possible to be this dead,
    and still be breathing, crying in my bed.

God please if you can hear,
    make it stop each and every tear.

God how could you be so cold,
    I'm lonely and I have nothing to hold.

Please God if you love me,
    let this pain let me be.

What is all this for,
    why is this my open door.

Big dreams,
    makes big pain gleam.

To build a character I need,
    I don't understand, inside I bleed.

God says trust,
    because the winds gust.

The bigger your destiny, the greater the storm,
    sit back and wait; a star is being born.

The world is in need of you,
    so just trust God in everything you do.

His Loss Our Gain

Nailed to the cross,
    we gained at His loss.

Through blood shed,
    King of the Jews the sign said.

As His perfect blood poured out,
    the Saints live to tell about.

His love, as He died for us,
    people made from dust.

The thorns pierced His head,
    to give us living bread.

As we eat and as we drink,
    we take, as we remember His last blink.

To live is to die and die is to live,
    to proclaim His love as we give.

Give ourselves as sacrifice,
   to the one who died and paid our price.

Cries of the Soul

BAD COMPANY

What kind of company are you keeping,
  what kind of unclean spirits are creeping.

The Bible clearly states,
  what the Lord hates.

But your inviting it into your gates, you want to be set free from sin,
  Choosing to be separate from the world is where to begin.

The world and God do not match,
  so take your soul and detach.

Let the spirit lead,
  in your every word, act and deed.

They will knock you down before you lift them up,
  what open doors got you trapped and stuck.

We need a common ground,
    so fruit can grow and be found.

A Holy life has no room,
    for destruction and doom.

So be watchful and discern,
    as you experience and learn.

Obey the Word,
    and strongholds will be cured.

To get out of your mess,
    trust God to restore and bless.

But you must change your people and things,
    because the consequences sting.

Life or death? It's your choice,
    it's your life, it's your voice.

Prosperity or defeat?
    Don't let failures repeat.

Do His will,
    and your cup he will fill.

Say no even if it hurts your heart,
    let your holy life start.

Cries of the Soul

THE ROOT

There is a cycle to pair,
    a reason it remains.

All the hurt, anger and tears,
    are just symptoms and fears.

You must get down to the root,
    to kill it, you must regroup.

What is it you're dealing with right now?
    Is it ugly and foul?

Rejection, anger, bitterness and hate;
    all inside, but it's not too late.

The issue at hand,
    there's a reason, its rooted in the sand.

To pluck,
    to get it unstuck.

You have to ask why you have this all inside,
    go back to your past; evaluate and resist pride.

What happened to you?
    Who broke your spirit? What did you go through?

The process has to be,
    definite to set you free.

Evaluate and respond,
    forgive, let go and move on.

Give your hurt to God, He will heal,
    your heart and every emotion you feel.

It's a process – clear out your mind,
    and let the healing power be divine.

Let Him touch every inch of your being,
    and you will send that root fleeing.

The symptoms will just fall off,
    and fruit will begin as your heart grows soft.

There's a work to be done,
    for your victory to be won.

Trust in God through thick and thin,
    Because He won't crush you, but He'll make you bend.

It's not easy; it is hard,
    but He will give you the trump card.

If you fall and trip,
    just remember, hold on with a tight grip.

Cries of the Soul

He is there, He will never let you go,
  sometimes it hurts to grow.

FORGIVE

Forgive! All offenses against you,
    Forgive! What they have put you through.

Don't let poison infect your heart,
    let anguish and bitterness depart.

You say they don't deserve the release,
    let the sickness cease.

Unforgiveness causes many things to arise,
    Disease and pain, I wouldn't advise.

Let it go; give it to the Spirits power,
    and quit being angry and sour.

Happiness is in forgiving everyone,
    healing is the reward done.

God is love, it is the secret in the sauce,
    it is the blood at the cross.

Cries of the Soul

Why hurt when you can give it away;
    this hour, this day.

He His peace engulf your soul,
    let the Spirit fill in the hole.

Eat the fruit,
    of a joy in pursuit.

Lay it down,
    and let it all be found.

THE CHURCH OF LACK

Lean not on your own understanding – that's what's in the Word,
   it's God breathed, it's the truth you heard.

All the debate,
   of what's true and false, because your mind can't create.

You don't understand so you call it a lie,
   you lack knowledge, so you accept satan's tie.

You have your own beliefs,
   told to you by the thief.

But still the truth remains,
   as many worship in vein.

The Spirit cannot reside,
   where the anti-Christ divides.

Cries of the Soul

The Church is dead,
    because you don't believe what you read.

You're in denial,
    as the winds are in spiral.

God's looking for an end time people,
    to manifest miracles in His steeple.

The bridge the gap for one accord,
    for a people who fear the Lord.

MY ENTRUSTED

Watch over my children with care,
    be just and fair.

I don't want Christian roots to soak the world's view,
    is not to be for my chosen few.

I've entrusted these little ones,
    to grow up with Spiritual guns.

I give you the inheritance of this child,
    train him up in my ways; lowly and mild.

The ways of the wise,
    have nothing in common with wicked flies.

Watch them as they grow,
    and let values flow.

Your household will be,
    blessed as I decree.

Cries of the Soul

Don't give in to their flesh,
    trust Me to bring out the best.

In this you must obey,
    raise my children right in this last day.

Your raising Heavens Army for Me,
    come with me and agree.

Where two are gathered it will be done,
    obey me as you raise my son.

Fire

I got the fire of the Holy Ghost,
    soaking as I roast.

This power has been made,
    sharp as a razor blade.

It is raining down,
    this power presence that I found.

This fire,
    my one desire.

It engulfs me like the sun engulfs the sky,
    the Holy Spirit is the reason why.

The Father and the Son,
    to empower me to get my work done.

A destiny full of vision,
    He's preparing me for my mission.

Cries of the Soul

This fire,
    what does it require?

It's all worth everything I give up,
    for the Spirit overflowing my cup.

This power I can't contain,
    the fire in the rain.

The presence I have found,
    rises up and is ground.

Where am I going?
    What light am I showing?

Obedience got me filled,
    grace got me healed.

Thank you Jesus for the fire that lives in me,
    I only ask for a hotter degree.

I want more,
    open up Heaven's door.

Release it into my soul,
    this fire; shake, rattle and roll.

Root it into my bones,
    as I shake and moan.

The Holy Spirit has a hold,
    as my destiny unfolds.

I Pray

I pray!
    Father, that I may.

Be accepted in your sight,
    that you strengthen me in this fight.

No one knows the heart wrenching,
    the pain in my quenching.

The terror I encounter by day and the horror by night,
    to keep this light burning bright.

I Pray!
    Father, that I may.

Be spared this thorn,
    so my bleeding heart won't be torn.

This agony and torturous pain,
    may it be slain.

Cries of the Soul

It is like getting my heart ripped out,
    but still Your who I sing about.

I pray that you heal me this day,
    I rebuke it; that's what I say.

Give me strength to carry,
    this burden I bury.

Cries of the Soul

INNER LONGING

In the depths of my soul,
    when this life takes a toll.

I dream of Heavens Gates,
    and I get sad I have to wait.

I think of the angels and his face,
    but then he reminds me of grace.

People are in need,
    I'm here as an extension to feed.

The hungry of the lost,
    to tell about the blood and the cross.

Inside I long,
    for Heavens where I belong.

I cry out,
    with a loud shout.

Cries of the Soul

God please move and bring,
    me to the angels that sing.

To Heaven's Gates that shine,
    where beauty and light combine.

Where joy resides,
    where laughter never subsides.

Don't leave me here,
    where sadness is near.

But He reminds me,
    to open my eyes and see.

This life is a gift,
    where seasons shift.

The good and the bad,
    so lift my head and don't be sad.

My hour is mourning is at an end,
    and my jubilee He'll send.

He says take a breath,
    and quit dreaming of death.

There's a reason you have to stay,
    revelations here today.

Clap your hands, give Me praise,
    glorious is my ways.

Take a stand,
    smile, grab onto My hand.

I'm taking you to that next place,
    where Earth can see My face.

Where fire comes down,
    Glory is the next round.

Say a prayer, shut your eyes,
    your spirit meets me in the skies.

Where we become one,
    where we play and run.

Open up your heart,
    that's where vision starts.

Come out into a whole new realm,
    where the camera never runs out of film.

This is a secret garden where spirits meet,
    where I wash your feet.

Sing and dance,
    fall into a dream like trance.

Tell the world it is time,
    to take a climb.

Tell them to get hungry enough,
    and my power I will stuff.

There's plenty in stock,
    for each and every rock.

Wake up open your eyes,
    it's not time for goodbyes.

THIS PLACE

As I gazed,
    the Spirit raised.

I've seen God's eye,
    I've seen the angels fly.

I stood at His Throne,
    I felt His embrace in the Glory Zone.

One touch and I was changed,
    my DNA was rearranged.

I'm coming into levels,
    I can sense diamonds, jewels and pebbles.

Just one embrace,
    left an imprint of pure taste.

I tasted and I've sees,
    the Glorious Presence, in a light beam.

I've seen God and I've seen Heaven's Gate,
   I've seen the mansion, all the Lords creates.

The music had such divine notes, so beautiful, the cloud of smoke.
   I went into healing, no longer was I broke.

Then I awoke and my eyes opened here,
   and I've seen my reflection in the mirror.

There is no place I'd rather be,
   than having you Lord, right beside me.

SIMPLICITY

As I sit in His mist,
    I am making a list.

The very things we sometimes forget,
    are the things that being writ.

Paying attention to the big & missing the small,
    were ignoring the most important of all.

Possessions, fame and wealth,
    when we should be thankful for health.

This life in it's simple form,
    keeps us safe in the storm.

The simplicity of gentle warmth in our soul,
    the love that fills the empty hole.

The Spirit we hold near,
    the small we hold dear.

Life and love, it is simple,
> the smile that brings dimples.

Family and friends;
> the sweet touch that descends.

The voice in the rain,
> the intimacy, not the fame.

A right heart cultivates,
> as the love of God creates.

Be thankful in the small,
> and then He will call.

The big thins to take place,
> but first see His face.

SHEOL

If you die and ascend to sheol,
    there is no more, let's make a deal.

The fire and the flames,
    are calling your names.

With every breath,
    God is pulling you to Him, so Heaven is your destiny
    at death.

Now is the time to decide,
    where your soul will reside.

There will come a day,
    when death will betray.

If you die and the fires of shoel,
    some as torment to feel.

It is forever, there is no break,
    that flame of hell has you in its lake.

Cries of the Soul

The screams of pain,
    and cries of help are in vein.

There's no longer a way out,
    no matter how loud the shout.

It will be over, demons will send plagues,
    as locusts eat the flesh from your legs.

They will beat you day and night,
    and your wreaked body won't be able to fight.

This life is where you have a choice,
    repent and let God hear your voice.

TRULY SAVED

There's many, who claim to be saved,
    but what has resurrected from your grave.

You can't be saved and live like the devil,
    you can't be a rebel.

Your heart must withstand change,
    your life must change lanes.

If your living like you always have,
    you have accepted lies from the crab.

The deceiver got over on you,
    this is all true.

To accept Jesus is to decide,
    to serve Him and be His bride.

To love His ways with all your heart,
    to let the old you depart.

God and the world have nothing to share,
    except spiritual warfare.

Stand up and close off the old,
    Let a new life unfold.

SOARING FOR HEALING

Tammy Henson

Available Everywhere Books Are Sold

Cries of the Soul

www.ingramcontent.com/pod-product-compliance
Lightning Source LLC
Chambersburg PA
CBHW070101080526
44586CB00013B/1148

William the Conqueror